PENTATONIX

ISBN 978-1-4803-7063-0

MADISON GATE RECORDS
FACEBOOK.COM/MADISONGATERECORDS

HAL•LEONARD®
CORPORATION
7777 W. BLUEMOUND RD. P.O. BOX 13819 MILWAUKEE, WI 53213

Visit Hal Leonard Online at
www.halleonard.com

AH-HA

Words and Music by
IMOGEN HEAP

Cost you to keep me qui - et.

THE BADDEST GIRL

Words and Music by AVI KAPLAN,
KEVIN OLUSOLA, KIRSTIE MALDONADO,
MITCHELL GRASSI, SCOTT HOYING
and BENJAMIN BRAM

Moderately, in 2

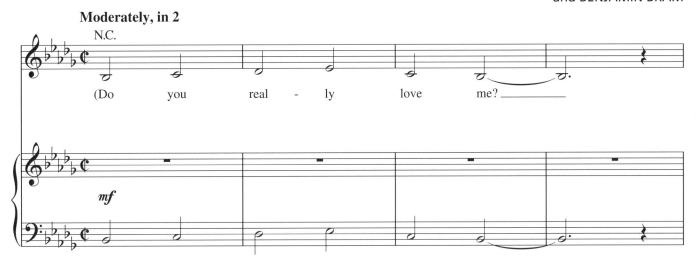

(Do you real - ly love me? ____

Do you real - ly care? ____

Do you real - ly want me? ____

14

HEY MOMMA/
HIT THE ROAD JACK

Words and Music by
PERCY MAYFIELD

I NEED YOUR LOVE

Words and Music by CALVIN HARRIS
and ELLIE GOULDING

42

RUN TO YOU

Words and Music by MITCHELL GRASSI,
SCOTT HOYING, AVI KAPLAN,
KIRSTIE MALDONADO, KEVIN OLUSOLA
and BENJAMIN BRAM

LOVE AGAIN

Words and Music by MITCHELL GRASSI,
SCOTT HOYING, AVI KAPLAN,
KIRSTIE MALDONADO and KEVIN OLUSOLA

LOVE YOU LONG TIME

Words and Music by JAZMINE SULLIVAN
and SALAAM REMI

Moderately, in 2

know I'm act-ing fool-ish. No-bod-y ev-er loved me.

No-bod-y ev-er loved me...

(...quite like you do).

Got a real girl, and she loves me a lot, and ain't no oth-er man is gon'

take-a my spot, and I, I'm so hap-py you're mine, and

NATURAL DISASTER

Words and Music by MITCHELL GRASSI,
SCOTT HOYING, AVI KAPLAN,
KIRSTIE MALDONADO and KEVIN OLUSOLA

_____ I'm bro - ken and hurt, _ and now I know _ it'd nev - er work. _ You see, I

tried. Hon - ey, oh, did _ I try. _____
(Oh, I tried.)

My soul, it died _ in Ar - ma - ged - don. My soul, it died, _ from your love, _

_____ from your love. _____ You're bring-ing these plagues on me.

SHOW YOU HOW TO LOVE

Words and Music by AVI KAPLAN,
KEVIN OLUSOLA, KIRSTIE MALDONADO,
MITCHELL GRASSI and SCOTT HOYING

(Let me show you how to...) (Whoa, _____ oh, _____ oh, _____ whoa,

oh, _____ oh. _____ (Ooh, _____

_____ ooh.) _____

This girl's got me fall-ing in love _____ and out of my mind. _____

STARSHIPS

Words and Music by NADIR KHAYAT,
ONIKA MARAJ, CARL FALK,
WAYNE HECTOR and RAMI YACOUB

Moderately fast

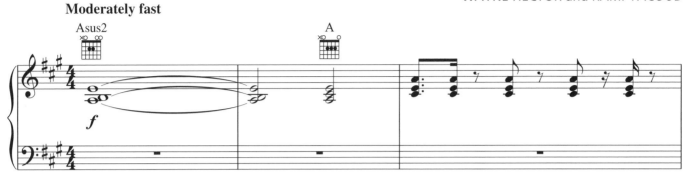

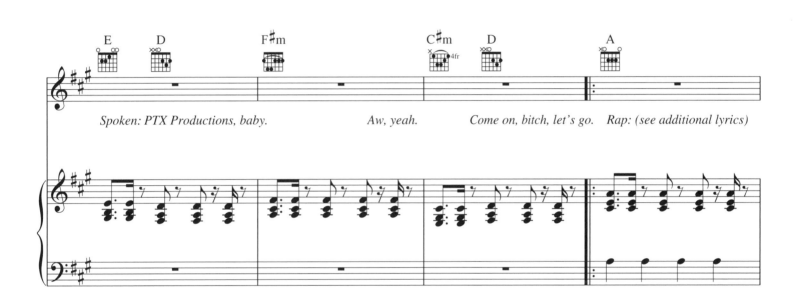

Spoken: PTX Productions, baby.   Aw, yeah.   Come on, bitch, let's go.   Rap: (see additional lyrics)

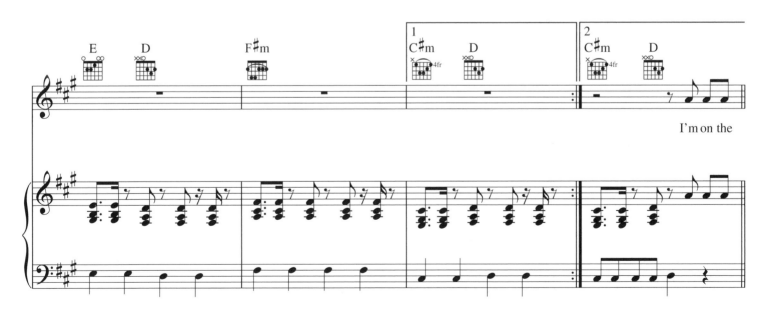

I'm on the

Additional Lyrics

Rap I: Let's go to the beach, each,
Let's go get a wave.
They say, what they gonna say?
Have a drink, clink, found the Bud Light.
Bad bitches like me is hard to come by.

The Patron, own, let's go get it on.
In the zone, own, yes, I'm in the zone.
Is it two, three? Leave a good tip.
I'm 'a blow all my money and don't give two shits.

Rap II: Now ev'rybody, let me hear you say ray, ray, ray.
Now spend all your money 'cause today's pay day.
And if you're a G, you're a G-G-G,
My name is Kirsten, you can call me Kirstie.

VALENTINE

Words and Music by SAMPHA SISAY,
JESSICA WARE and TIMMAZ ZOLLEYN

WE ARE YOUNG

Words and Music by JEFF BHASKER,
ANDREW DOST, JACK ANTONOFF
and NATE RUESS